FROST FYRE

and Other Poems

Flossie Benton Rogers

Moonspell Books

Moonspell Books

Dedication

To my childhood and forever friend
Meg,
thank you for keeping a notebook of
my poems safe and sound.

In memory of my beloved husband,
Ronnie—always and forever.

For my brave, talented son, Ashley,
who keeps me living in the light.

Foreword

This collection extends over time, and reviewing poems for possible inclusion brought up deep feelings and energies. For the most part, it was a positive and stimulating experience—but not always. Still, having the words, giving voice to the emotions, has always been a gift of grace that outweighs the pain. Besides, how wonderful that we as humans plunge the depths and scale the summits.

Putting poems in print is not an easy or natural thing to do. It had me quaking in my boots more often than not. The thought of others judging such personal and down to the bone expression is downright scary. So—one more bugaboo vanquished!

Come with me to the inner worlds of Frost Fyre. Journey to a realm where all time is now, the soul is eternal and multi-dimensional, and gods and goddesses walk among us.

Contents

FROST FYRE
and Other Poems
Flossie Benton Rogers
Copyright © 2018

FROST FYRE

Nightfall

in a winter grotto

carved

by North Wind's

cheeks

secluded from din

She beckons guardians

opens pathways

chanting words

fraught with meaning

drawing spirit threads

through portals

to weave a sacred space

between moments

allowing the whispers

of gods and angels

to enter this world

on all the channels

Magic calls

DENDRA

We speak to stars

you and I.

We gaze rapt

till stardust

fills our eyes,

and shimmering stardust

spills our hair upon the waves.

Proteus' rubied staff

will roll no more.

I see bones upon the shore,

and yet the bones are still—

bleached by starlight

bleached and blinding

in the dark.

Thin

long fingers

brush silver

deep cold black

stars

YURII

Winter branches swaying from icy gusts
of north wind's cheeks,
barren branches, alone and desolate.
Far out upon the snow-covered meadow
a rabbit scurrying after something lost.
What is lost but spring and yellow flowers
for my table?
Winter white displaces it all, and more.
Glistening swirls and magic icy patterns
upon my pane,
with a small breath become clear for
viewing.
It is a white winter
of blended sounds and sights,
and blended destinies.

OCTOBER

October, with her black satin
eyes, came flashing into
autumn, her midnight hair
streaming behind by Zephyr's
wildness, her long orange dress
fluttering about her
body, her lips singing Maenad songs
to the trees. Thus she came,
and laughed with the moon.

TO THE OLD GODS

There is something

wild

in the air.

The moon is large

and yellow

and beats in rhythm with my soul.

The ancient gods

gaze

at the moon,

and then turn to me

with tender eyes.

They do not understand

my long love,

but are grateful.

And they know

I shall never forget

the ancient songs.

BOIL

Hot music

from the dark womb

bore us

from the Mother's

dark womb

long ago

before us

before time

she spit us out

red and juicy

pomegranate seeds

on a breath

a steaming cry

a hiss that seared the night

now

Earth the Mother

nears her

time

once more

FRIAR'S LANTERN

We are quicksilver,

ignis fatuus in some god's dream,

flitting from the primeval womb

to the dark forest

to carved stone

and the steel tomb

in less than a sigh.

Little doubt

that our agonized shouts

are imperceptible

to that vast ear

accustomed to waltzes of planets

and litanies of stars.

Are we splats of bright color

unstable in the mind

like an unformed thought?

A minor indiscretion?

Shall we,

forgotten,

disappear in the slow-moving,

ever-revolving

vastness of universes?

RHEA

We seek you, Mother

through the man-maze

of time,

forward and backward

to the magic now,

the open egg of you,

the great beating heart of you

that measures love

not time.

Peeling

away layers of

his-story,

we breathe your woman smell

in wild places

where moondrops

fall

gold on spiral dancers,

where sprays of mist

on craggy rocks near the sea

drench

the rapt

drench the very cells

so that now

NOW

we remember

you Mother

BONE WOMAN

Bone woman
haunches strong
feet clutched
roots
seeking blood fire below
nourishment rising
flowing
flooding
the loins of
Bone Woman
hair witched
eyes wild
palms open
to hold the moon

TO MY HUSBAND

This is a poem for my husband Ronnie
whom I have loved time
out of mind
whose dark and penetrating soul eyes
touch a deep place within me
where cool jeweled waters
lick sun-incensed rocks
our grotto secret
and ripe with magic, Adam and Eve
when we were others.
From lovers
to enemies—
teeth bared and
circling—
to lovers again,
you were there with your eyes
and I knew you knew
you were mysteriously mine.
And now I see you are

the magician, whose knowledge

arcane tempts

from the very edge of eternity

all the women I have been

and so I capture you here,

you,

my always husband Ronnie,

my beloved.

DEMETER

Thank you, Mother,

for filling spaces

and kneading the surface to mud

a child's finger swirls

and needs the murky goo

your pelt provides.

Mud woman

sodden earth woman

let's play in the mud

let's follow

and sink down

and down

and down

to the core

ISIS

The Mother's
blood and bones
seep into me
relentlessly
and without remorse
until I am blood-full
and holy
silent as dusk
as I hold the sacred baby
death
in my arms
so powerful
so rare

WHITE SUN AND MOUNTAIN

All

was the spirit that moved in the darkness;

Within

him countless images lay safely.

Suddenly

his soul flashed with rainbows of light,

a drastic change from night's ethereal ice.

Freely he chose the

knifing agony of

suffering and death to

create becoming.

Spreading through the universe

in many forms;

the primal Mother and source of

pain and joy;

Stars, rain, swirling wind that brings the

sweet

rose scent—

Bound as one in eternity is it

All.

CERRIDWEN

The face in the mirror

has no eyes

just flaps of skin

and tiny holes

where eyes should be

in the rightness of the world

I remember

having eyes at birth

so—what happened?

Did someone pluck them out?

Were they stolen

eaten like Jaguar's blueberries?

Did they see

too much and pop out

plums come to life?

Did they see nothing

wither, wrinkled, disappear?

What happened?

What transpired?

I have a blankness.

Sisters, are you here?

I see a moronic face.

How can I see?

Not just blind

sightless

but completely eyeless

I less than anyone

Know

CLARE OF ASSISI

Clare sought God

in gold-rimmed clouds

and a kitchen full of scrubbed potatoes,

in Francis' ashes

and fire's repast.

A free woman

found a mother's breast

in father's sackcloth.

Subterranean

fire and water

rocked Clare

throughout the whole

serene turbulent

dream

of her life

PERSEPHONE

Control
slips away
like tears in the rain
releases the bile
choking the throat
piercing the heart
convulsing the belly.
Way down deep
wormy fear
crawls out,
sizzling the sun.
The picture
held so close
unravels
loses focus
fades and re-forms
motion
without end

INDUBITABLY JUNG

I plunged a knife into her heart; God, what
a heart!
She bled the berry red of the not so very
buried.
So I waited.
She fled through the night like Hecate
or like a Maenad with purple lips,
the silver moon silvering the shadows.
She had wanted a ready burning tear
for the wind's ecstasy
and the soul's joy,
and for that long-lost golden lover.
She was a witch;
she screamed revenge
for the moon is twins.
And she has it in a stone.

REGINA

I will go to him

should his fine clean fingers beckon

his burning eyes find mine

for an instant

a millisecond

dropped into the cauldron

where it stirs

bubbles

cosmic broth

I will go to him

should his wind-body beckon

spread out among the stars

less than air

less than stardust

the great nothing

I will go

REGINA ARRESTED

I remembered you—

oddly—

incompletely as a god

Apollo whole

and longed for you

as him

to take me

knowing full well the impossibility

(Leda is a man's story).

And you

as him

tarnished earth

but I learned to live with it.

I learned to love it

and move with the leaves in the sun,

and a quaking boldness forced me on.

And then

like a bolt of lightning—

see Zeus got me anyway—

you came surging up from dreams

and appeared on earth

silver in the dark

gold in the sun.

I know you

from all our yesterdays and times gone.

Miracles do happen:

we

one

REGINA REAL

What element

what enzyme

what ether-flown mystery

sparks recognition in me

of you,

transmutes

into woman, wife, mother

the peripheral now,

Inanna descending.

And yet crystallizes

forever

the alchemic moment

into time's art

into god's art.

Real are the dreams.

MEMPHIS

pale-shrouded

Ptah

of the dark and the full

of shadow and light

the slain bull—bleeding

who cannot lie or stand

at the no-time

when time is not

renews

from Nature within

Parzival later must earn the renewal

And on the fifteenth night

speaks the holy word

creating all from the word

And on Ptah

rests the heart of Egypt

TARTARUS

We stumble through

the shared delirium of daylight,

pale shades shuffling

in the weird dim day.

We are madder than the psychotic

with the cadaverous grin,

with our merry antics to hide

the hollow pit within.

Enough this, enough that,

enough anything—to hide the pit,

to hide the pit.

Lest we unmoor like Semele and float

toward Pluto and beyond,

succumbing to stark, crazed laughter,

or bearing the weight of paralytic freedom.

And how to move again?

How to do just one antic

out of the vast array of antics?

Is love of the pit

love for the weird dim day

and the pale shades shuffling?

SELENE

Silver light
the night's crescent eye
it's four in the morning
four past midnight
a misty four
moist and cooler
before you pale from sight
we lost you until the night
waning silver light
eye of the goddess
born on the wind
reigning of earth and sky
and stars in the night
woman is witch
witch is goddess
goddess is woman
the night
and silver light

SESHAT

The elephants of Tsavo

destroyed grandmother trees

trampled and chewed them

senselessly

despite our horror

and desire to manage death.

Later we found

the soil replenished

nourished by grandmother

and life teeming

above and below.

What do the elephants of Tsavo

know

that we don't know?

THE NEED OF MAEVE

Maeve looked on Cuchulain

and found him fair

with combs of jasper she pulled up her

hair and bound her loins in jewels

Macha's scent dampened her throat

and the beating hollow of her breasts

Thus she readied herself for Cuchulain

A crescent moon swathed a path

to the lady's abode

curiously the steed pranced

Soon an immensity filled the door

shadowed the moon

and dancing candles

Maeve burned

as did Cuchulain

Her need poured and seared his soul

transmuting his gut to water

He left

unable to bear the intensity

Maeve

alone in her chambers

plots the birth of Cuchulain

MERITATEN

I saw you walking, Mother,

quickly,

peering around,

clenching something beneath your cape,

away from the place

my father lay.

Afterwards

you said nothing—

but your eyes

met mine,

and knew.

And our silence

embalms

my father's house.

LACHESIS

Gossamer webs

woven low among grasses

wet shimmer in earth's morning breath

jeweled remnants of immortal dance.

Small feet

dishevel

the fabric of chaos

to form in abandoned play

a pattern of bright threads

against the dark.

Lachesis dances

silver attired

her Helen-like form

rapt in song.

She disavows

all but the skein

and each winding thread

solidifies the net.

AT THE NO-TIME

Just to hang on for a while.

Not to succumb to the little now

that tries, like maddening flies,

to obstruct my eyes,

to fill my vision with inconsequential

lies.

Damn it! I do care

that a child drops dead,

bloated eyes and bloated stomach

and the flies swarm—

that a thousand corpses lie

piled aside in foaming aberration

while people stare—

that governments buy

incredible weapons and,

pointing them at one another,

hold a billion lives in their sweaty hands.

Oh, but when I wrench my eyes

from the ballpark peephole

and turn them around inside,

the ages merge,

and sometimes

all coheres

in radiance.

SAMHAIN REVEL

We cry to the old ones who rest in our
bones,
in our hearts and blood,
stirring them to action.
Come and be with us, share the feast,
as dark mantles the earth,
and the cold wind rises.
Sit at your table where the candle flickers.
This bread and wine are for you,
as the toast, and the cheer,
and the old songs from the honeycombed
walls.
The moon shall never
neglect a traveler
or a secret whispered on a hallowed night.

ARTEMIS TO DENDRA

Let me reveal
myself.
Let us walk in the grove
silent and unforthcoming,
darkness deep within our skin,
let us walk for a long time
until the moon rises,
and then,
let my radiance
touch you,
your face turn,
and your eyes widen
of what cannot be known
by words
acts
or thoughts of man.

ASTARTE

White foam splays where rain pounds the
water.
Entranced, I press my brow to the pane.

The cold soothes my fever, breaking the
storm inside me.
I am part of it all, after all.

Behind me the office continues to bustle.
Only man can be alone.

Now the wind whips the pane with its icy
lashes.
Words are lost in the sea and the wind.

In the churning black mist, I can't tell
where the sky ends.
I fly to the water, and rise from the foam.

GRACE

The moon stirs me and stars transmute,

and the cooling wind changes eye and ear

to mouth.

Even the Orphean eye

is enough to justify Adolph Tantalus

and Soames the dry Forsyte;

I am mesmerized and learn to love.

As the Orphean ear engages

I am lifted to the heights below graves,

the sacred place where two are one,

home of Tiresias, and Seth and Horus.

When the Orphean mouth opens

I am regal and alone,

but stir and transmute with moon and stars

and thus am all.

LILITH

Between Eve the hollowed gourd

Eve on her bottom

circumcised and banished from the garden

by a prudish god

and half-dead men,

and a witch-woman storming

bleeding and lusty

who surges in the night

bearing torches to light the moon

and sear the dead

free and wild

radiant with rage

I choose Lilith

THE CHAPEL PERILOUS

An old, insipid moon
shines wanly down
on hard, dark rock,
where once the morning mist
spilled over farm and wood.
It was a wet world then.
Things moved in the wet.
From the staggering deer
among leaf piles
to the farm cat lapping cream.
To the farmer's wife brewing coffee.
One purple eastern streak
stretched far and away in love-hate:
the ultimate emotion,
as Orin or the Boleyn could say,
toward the stirring, sterling, comforting
cup—
one drink and then you're out.

ODE TO RAIN

Cold rain, icy rain,

for you alone I tarry

in ecstatic pain.

You have loosed once more,

from heaven's watchful eye come

to permeate my core.

Or hell's fiery pits?

Whence you sped fervently

to tear my soul to bits.

Rain, I thirst for you.

I have great need of you.

That you've come is just enough

to make life worth the while.

RHIANNON

moon wings I have and soul fire of my
own
despair I know not
fear is beyond me
on wings of angels I ride forth to the light
hear me in the mourning dove hear me at
night
hear the banshee cry to silence those who
listen
come with me ride the wild wind
curl your toes upon my broom
hide not from me fear not
I am closer than even you know
Iris Delily abalone shells
Io dancing at the well
I fled the bravo of heroes
I come to you now in silence and prayer
the flute of the soul
watery time blessings arise

Aradia sister

Tuesday spell Ananthe at the cistern well

spell

time to choose which task to perform

which chest to open

in the night of the soul

myriad patterns on snow in the dark

singing

go into the silence

we come to love

you are the core of the world

shrink not

the path before you is light

WEST OF THE MOON

West of the moon darkness lies,
behold sadness and horror
within her black eyes.
To glimpse in silent shadows
of her melancholy eyes,
fate and eternal woes.
One can only be aware;
the sun and light are gone and
the experience is rare.
Both are Nature—joy and darkness;
death is a final returning
to the moon's warm breast.

EURYDICE

High upon the jagged cliff she knelt
in the raging storm,
Above her was nothing but vagueness
and she yearned for it,
She felt close to the many voices
singing there,
Faintly she could hear the chattering
from the ground below,
Dimly she could see the clearness
and many people,
They seemed not to notice how far away
she was from them,
and kept speaking as if she could hear
and love the clearness,
Then in the crystal pond below
she saw her image,
and realized it was this to
which they were speaking,
Suddenly her entire body

lurched downward,

So that she was partly hanging

over the cliff's edge,

This effort to hear the chattering

was not fulfilled,

The singing voices grew louder

as she died...

EPONA TO ARES

Could you be who I am seeking?
The wind rustling through trees,
and the rain,
an icy whiteness in the eternal
black.
A oneness with my heart and with Nature.
I have searched so long,
waiting to love you. Needing
you for my ethereal journeys.
Needing to experience your
journeys, too, in a world
without time.
The cold rain falls on our
fingertips;
will they touch in a moment
of eternity?

AUTUMN ODE

There are no words I
can give to you, for all
are meaningless.
I can offer no worldly
riches, nor promises.
Deep pain breathes jaggedly
in my soul.
Before me are your eyes,
spirited with the forest,
reflecting my image.
My gifts for you are of the moon—
cool October rain that brings
remembrance,
leaves of red and amber rustling in the
wind,
a green sea surging ever closer.
We have need of all this, in our
transient, eternal love.

BRISEIS TO ACHILLES

Old in winters, I call to you,
Achilles of the swift feet,
to unite your ethereal tune
with mine.
As twilight of the silvery
fingers slips silently
about the rustling leaves,
I hear your voice in sweet
melancholy strains,
upon the soft kisses of Zephyr.
As the last shreds of darkness
descend upon earth,
our two voices shall glide
toward the moonlight,
singing.

CAVE OF HECATE

dark and wild

renew the child

once the wind howls

once the flame burns

once the sea rises

burst open the seed of your belly

dark goddess

and free the light

TO GOLDMUND

Glowing white icy fire,

touch my hand

in painful desire.

Goldmund, speak your heart to me,

in wordless

songs of eternity.

I plead, beg from deep within,

do not let

me die before I've been.

See fair autumn's amber leaves,

hear icy green

that no one believes.

Sweep me up to dawning's breath;

then I will

faithfully welcome death.

MORRIGAN

No sweet sad death for me.
Agony seeking, the grinning
grave floats closer, looming
clear before my eyes.
Tear my soul from my body,
bit by bit, acute pain,
clasp my heart in your
ugly teeth. Yet, in
sweet eternal sadness I
contemplate a falling leaf
or dying cricket. Which shall
I reconcile to the other?

AENGUS

Emanating from your eyes and your
wind-blown hair is youth, green-
misted, fleeting youth, captured
eternally within those stormy eyes that
gave birth to images—
raging rain blown wild by the wind,
foaming tumultuous sea,
silver moonlight streaming silently and
cool. Immortality breathes
of poetry in your eyes.

RIDDLE

Why do we speak such meaningless words
to each other? Words of wisdom should
be spoken, eternal words that exist within
themselves. Even wordless words. We
have so little time! And yet you ask,
"How are you?" and I reply, "Fine."

SKADI

We are alone

amidst the white night,

but why are we weeping?

Faraway, wolves howl

in the moonlit

wooded winter.

No time

have we for sadness.

That will come

soon enough.

Then,

the barren icy

branches shall

droop lower,

as snow covers

our blended souls.

PHAETHON

Explosions of brilliant color,

he spreads his fingers to the sky,

striving to hear the whispering,

upward to thinner air,

gasping

in the blackness.

Blending of ancient souls

and needs,

in this remote region.

One breath of sadness and joy,

painful fusion of greenness

and death.

Transitory, yet

eternal,

lost again and again, forever.

CASSANDRA

Sunlight warming the cold earth,

fingers stretching toward my darkened fortress,

lonely blackness without mirth.

And wordless here I have fled,

in silent tears, for they understand not

what is longing to be said.

The world in all entirety

is sun to them, the contrast between us,

illusion which I can see.

For the sight I did not ask,

the burden upon me dark and heavy,

questioning, an endless task.

Yet, in my sorrow I smile,

the road is winding with worthy ribbons,

and the moon is mine a while.

ODE TO RONNIE

Winter twilight descends upon tree

branches,

white and snow covered.

Alone in the forest, feeling the anguish

of your silent voice…

how I long

to bear your pain, to give you love.

Faraway is a tiny flicker

in a cottage window, a candle shedding

tears,

awaiting someone.

Winter shadows fall upon the naked

whiteness,

painful shadows

of our blendedness.

PLEA

Moon of silver waning glisten,

soft upon my lover's eyes,

pull us close that we might feel

the raining of the night.

Primal woodland streaming music,

wet upon the natal leaves,

let us listen as the stars

are dreaming in the sky.

Rain that brings eternal magic,

wet and cool upon our lips,

fuse our bodies with your touch

to save our love from death.

THE SUN

He saw the sun rise above the sea,
slowly with red stretching yawns,
bringing the earth greenness and singing
birds.
Throughout the day he watched the god
gliding across the sky,
smoldering and mighty in his great fire-
chariot.
He was still looking as the flame-haired
grew sleepy
and slipped into the sea gently,
soaking his tired body in the cool water;
And the man lay silent in the night.

LEAVES

Whither I shall ever wander
among the greens and scarlet reds,
and merge with every swirling leaf
who finds the earth its final home;
Racing along the meadow swiftly
as icy rain wets our face,
its silver ancient frenzied tears
beating downward upon the earth,
Into the forest with the music
of primal times and forgotten night,
songs of spirits mad and wild,
dancing beneath the rising moon,
A silver glow and trembling leaves
bring the end of maenad dreams,
but I will know where I have been
for remembered greens are ever so.

SONNET II

When we were young and fresh we never
dreamed
that time could pass and youth and beauty
fade,
Upon his golden throne fair Phoebus
seemed
to shrink from sinking down to rest and
shade.
While in the air enchanting lilac scent
spread far about the greenest hill and dale,
And violets sweet did all their fragrance
vent
upon the fiery winds of Phoebus' sail.
But withered cold and dead the lilac hangs
now like the violet covered with white,
While Phoebus chooses sleep to winter
pangs,
Selene about us sheds her ancient light.
Days of golden youth are old and gone,

And the icy moon shivers all alone.

TO RONNIE

More than the wind softly sighing

through nocturnal clusters of leaves,

More than the tumbling of raindrops

as rose-scented strains of a lyre,

More than the shimmers of moonlight

on tremulous, golden waters—

I love you.

KYRENE

When I look at Selene,

white ice-fire of the sky,

I feel that somewhere close

is Apollo of the golden locks,

walking sandal-footed among the misted

trees,

his eyes softly set

on one he loves,

his blithe arms open to embrace her

and me.

OMEGA

As I stood on the pavement,

I seemed to see the ages roll by,

one upon the other.

I saw the cement crack and break,

slowly, neglected,

and dissolve into dust.

I saw lost hollow eyes

and bony figures quaked with cold;

and these slipped away like shadows.

Then words and images faded,

and were gone.

And even, oh even the long bare trees

stopped,

as the moon plunged into the icy sea.

And now, in the black cold there is

nothing,

no trace. No trace.

IT IS MADDENING

It is maddening to think that

when one is dead, one is dead.

That the flesh rots, is eaten,

that clear eyes and a tender smile

are nothing.

Back to the earth, to the beginning,

for the body.

But merely the body?

Is there nothing more?

I am one with Apollo,

wild Dion, and the soft-eyed Chloe,

with Akhenaten, Amon-Ra,

and the swift running Nile.

But does it signify?

RONNIE

More than you seek to know me,

I seek to know you,

for the wind is rustling through your hair,

and I also love its caresses.

I have need of you,

of your rain and roses,

for I too know

that rain ceases and roses die.

As the wind is touching you,

so do I wish to touch,

a blending of souls,

a gathering of worthiness.

God of the rain,

singing clearly and cool,

as moonlight streaming

onto white forest leaves,

while I, a mere fragment,

lie groping in darkness;

yet I love the darkness

as well as I love the moon.

HECATE

Sing Hollow Men,

of the cavern where Hecate dwells,

that lonely spot west of the sun,

beyond its warmth and brightness,

that dark spot far from the moon,

whose silver cloak that soothes many

shuns this, Hecate's abode.

Feel the cold teeth of the night,

endless cold

that tears the flesh

and gnaws the marrow of the bone.

Breathe the aroma

tinting the air,

a strange night blossom

that neither grows nor wilts.

Hear the wind wailing

outside the cavern,

so mournful a sound,

the only music of this dwelling.

Taste the draft

from Hecate's cup,

a bitter potion that numbs the brain

and burns the soul with despair.

See the goddess Hecate

in her dark, loathsome cavern,

a tall form enclosed in ebony,

black hair flowing, head slightly bowed.

See her face both new and old,

a strange face, foul and comely,

and green eyes in gazing sorrow

for the lone fate that is hers.

Sing, Hollow Men,

of Hecate the witch,

who lives the melancholy of the world

in her lost, eternal cavern.

Sing throughout the ages

of this woman's sorrow,

of one who lives her destiny

within the shadows of the earth.

IN OCTOBER

The wild October zephyr

surges

in age-old rhythms,

gold and scarlet leaves

swirl from the sky

and frisk along the ground,

the long night

pulsates

with tiny silver sparkles,

and a clean chill pervades the air,

suddenly my pace quickens

as the cold purple sea

lashes

about my bare feet.

I hurry on.

TO JOHN KEATS

Warm scribe

that wrote of mysterious spices and juicy

plums

which wet the lips with delight,

of mountain laurel and soft winds

havening a winged youth and his love,

of feeble, grey-stricken Saturn

and the weeping queen,

old gods in a new time—

touch me,

enclose my fingers in an embrace

that destroys the grave.

FOR THESEUS

The autumn wind blows raw and chilled

with forgotten songs and scents—

Ariadne weeping by the sea,

the rose breath of Hippolyta's hair,

magic memories of an old time when the

blond Achaean

moved the stone.

THE ATLANTEAN SCOPS

Backward to a faraway time,

past Yeats and Keats,

past Spenser,

even long beyond Homer,

backward—

in a time jeweled with ruby and sapphire

walk the poets of the forgotten world,

their words gone,

their names lost forever,

their shining eyes

conjured

by my memory.

APOLLO'S PRIESTESS

Many times

I knelt before the offering,

chanting sacred words

to your presence,

as did those before me

and those after;

But I loved you more,

my lips caressed your name

in holy whispers,

my tears fell

at the thought of your pain;

And now,

after all the unknown time

it is the same.

PHILONA NEAR ELEUSIS

You lay on the coarse bedding

after the battle,

while I dressed your wounds

and smoothed oils

over your battered body.

And then, beneath silver stars,

the sweet wine and playful whispers

eased your pain

and stirred fires within us.

Your strong shoulders above me,

your wine lips on mine,

urgency rose

and our bodies flowed

on the silver music of Poseidon.

DUSK

As dusk slips over the day,

a widow's veil,

the earth trembles.

the ground chills,

and the air becomes a mist

of shadows,

some darker than others,

all shadows.

Color disappears.

No more red and yellow.

No more green.

Sing, whippoorwill,

the earth is waiting

for your night song,

sing, lone herald,

and men must listen

within their houses.

THE MIDNIGHT MOON

The moon rose at twelve o'clock
and Simona saw it rise.
What startled her awake so late
that moisture burned her eyes?
Could it be a fiendish ghost
or ghoul that broke her sleep?
In any case the little girl
threw off the quilted heap
and to the window, slowly, softly,
eased her tiny frame,
a curious child, to know the truth
her bold but fear-filled aim.
Her ruffled nightgown swishing on
the newly shining floor
she climbed upon the window seat
and gazed at Nature's store.
The silver waning midnight moon
transfixed her as a stone
and though no one was up but she,

she was not alone.

The amethyst eyes of Selene

smiled upon the child,

and every aromatic scent

was swept in—from the wild.

The shining goddess touched her face

and hummed an ancient song;

the wind and all the flowers and trees

began to sing along.

Asleep once more in her bed

Simona fell to dream,

and all the myriad figures sang

the ivory lady's theme.

A POET IS A MYSTERY

1

A poet is a mystery:

Now cold and firm

but subject still

to the indentations of fingertips.

Now tepid and shapeless,

a mountain brook

meandering toward its destination,

then gaining speed near the end.

Grape-scented,

loving the wooded hills of Naxos

and the tingling cool of the racing stream.

Delicious,

ready to be eaten.

But hungry still

2

So hungry—

for the white stars of the night
that pulsate blue and red

for the unknown dark worlds—
their music flows
in familiar strains—

for the wind,
rustling, raging, omnipotent father

for the green of trees
and the yellow of jonquil

for the western moon

for Ariel
and the Red Crosse Knight
and Crazy Jane

for Goldmund
and the Wife of Bath

and Yurii Zhivago

3

The nightingale sings in China

"Is there no rest for the weary?"
The grandmother sighs.
"When will the top stop spinning?"
asks the child.

4

What can the poet say about the moon?

HECUBA

They have imprisoned me
in walls of stone,
no door or window,
nor the dimmest ray of light,
Only bitter black and cold stone—

I recall things,
images flow,
A field of fragrant phlox
cannot be lovely now
in the face of the wolf gnawing at the
flesh.
Poor phlox
that know not of pain,
Happy phlox—

The child in the womb
cannot bring comfort

in the face of the wolf gnawing at the
flesh,
The child will be gnawed as well,
How is it possible
not to know of the snarling wolf?

Apollo has gone,
his lyre an unthinkable thought,
Again, a child betrayed—
How it is possible?
How is it possible?

Alone,
Only bitter black and cold stone,
And the wolf takes my throat

JOURNEYING

I lay upon the earth one summer morning,

flat and stretched out and lazy,

allowing warmth to seep into me,

and suddenly I began to grow large,

warmth filled me and I was vast,

vast and slow,

frightened by the space around me,

space larger than I,

nothing to hold me,

floating, frightened of falling,

but trusting in the ages,

trusting and vast and slow.

LONE ROB

Lone Rob plows the fields

in the golden green Kinraddie spring,

singing joy,

as his neighbors, but that his joy is more

than joy,

and less,

more human and less human,

the joy of a tree

and the heating earth beneath his feet.

When the night winds blow in

the distant sea,

Rob sits on a step,

his feet caressing cool dirt,

and sings sorrow,

the deep sorrow of the stars

and winter rain.

BRIEF INSIGHT INTO MATTERS PHYSICAL

Each of us holds up the earth with our feet,
how heavy the weight,
how terrifying the space beneath our
heads.

THE GOLDEN MAN

The Golden Man rose from the sea,

ankle-deep, gigantic,

his metallic body gleaming

with the light of a thousand suns,

his eyes arrowing cool blue shafts;

Tremble, and cast your puny bodies to the

ground—

the Golden Man has come.

FUSION

I feel the coolness of the wind amid the
raindrops
and gasp at the unparalleled beauty of
Orion,
What was separate is now one,
What divided has rearranged itself into
flowing rhythm,
The words of Keats are the rain—
words engendered in primal feeling
but working through and rising out of
complexity,
And only one who has experienced that
sad, unbearable knowledge
can see the utter core of the world,
or gaze into Apollo's eyes.

YOUNG JOLYON

I recall a winter morning
colder than any before,
Icicles clung to bare limbs
and frost whitened the world,
The air stung the skin
and numbed the fingers red,
The cold was so much so
that it was audible—
like music—
or like a friend,
One could speak to it,
I can feel it
even now—
just a touch—
in this summer rain.

THE MONK

Yesterday

in another life

I sat before the yellowed manuscript,

hot tallow dripping subtle sculpture

long into night,

tired eyes burning in awe

at the figure of Apollo,

a wrinkled hand

caressing

golden-fluttering dreams.

CREUSA

1

Terror,

someone crushing the breath from me,

I am only a little girl

only a child

and am falling in the blackness,

dying

2

Starchy sheet beneath me,

like a biology class earthworm—

long and stretched and done to—

jerking awake at the edge of sleep,

mouth moving rhythmically in the night

in unison with

that tiny rhythmic stranger

3

My arms—for his terror

and my breast—for his hunger,

darkness releases its soothing sphere

and I rest—in the warmth

of waking dreams

ON POETRY

So many passions breathe within me—

North Wind blasting—

that I could die from passion.

I could burst like a firecracker

into rainbows—

like Daniken's god

into rainbows—

Hold back the surging,

try to sigh,

catch the baseball before it drops

at third,

pull the rope on the balloon

spurt out each color one—

at a time.

CINQUAIN 1

Ashley
dimpled, chubby
giggles at play
tugging my mouth into
grins

CINQUAIN 6

pockets
isolated, dark
breathe of mystery
colder and colder than
winter

CINQUAIN 11

Ronnie

warrior-strong

touches my cheek

absorbing my tears with

love

CINQUAIN 40

Hecate

priestess, witch

collects juicy toads

waiting for the Mother's

moon

CINQUAIN 57

baby

tiny, ignorant

lay quite usual

metamorphosing later ice fire

Keats

CINQUAIN 81

John

aesthetic, fiery

paints morning gold

sacrificial pyre of the

Baptist

CINQUAIN 105

moon

full, golden

startles the senses

hanging eerily in morning

West

CINQUAIN 120

pigs

noisy, filthy

suck their mash

to be tomorrow packaged

slices

CINQUAIN 143

age
treacherous, tutelary
slithers, slips, creeps
cavorting toward the moldy
grave

CINQUAIN 203

Annis
wizened, sly
guards the portal
slicing the world from
dreams

SONG TO AUTUMN

Far distant blue clouds

of coming twilight

vibrating in passion,

Lone melodious wood thrush

skittering

against the sky,

Tree of age

with moss hanging

shedding silent tears,

Wind, sweet Zephyr,

hint of mystery

in your autumn chill,

into one eternal moment

these autumn auras fuse,

and are mine.

KITTEN IMPRESSIONS

Green is the ground
and the mauve-colored kitten
purrs at my feet. Briskly
upward I walk, but time
goes slowly. Backward glances
seem to bring him closer.
The ground floats with the
soft white covering.
Atop the hill I smile
back at the taffy
bundle sitting in the snow.

ANU

I saw you for the first time

in a long time

Father, my Father,

since I came into the dark space,

the inside out

crying place,

wound tight

ticking and spinning a mile a minute.

Just a glimpse,

the kind that burns the brain

with beauty.

You were not as I had known.

Not gold-shimmering

Apollo,

nor the fisherman

on the level shore.

But an older

stronger power

from the dark

wet

unruly deep—

more beautiful than breath.

Your dark eyes

how they glittered:

a thousand diamonds,

a thousand stars.

Black star eyes

that seemed to promise…

something…

unknown.

As yet unbirthed.

As yet…

unbirthed.

ZEUS

The bronze chamber lies beneath the
ground
a tomb, lonely, silent, and cold,
until a day when through the roof the
sound
of thunder roars, and the girl is awed to
behold
within the room a glistening shower of
gold;
verdurous glory will be the refrain
for the seed of the god of the golden rain.

RAGNAROK

It is here.

The smell of rain

the darkening leaves

the cool ground throbbing to burst.

The wind picks up a little.

Children quieten,

uneasy at dusk.

Birds listen in the forest,

along the pulsating sea.

Darker

the first distant stars flicker,

a blue moon hangs

on the horizon.

The earth lurches drunkenly

in her womb.

GUTHRUM THE DANE

As Volsung vowed glory

so do I – Guthrum – vow,

for the sparrow flies swiftly

through the room.

Weary over wintry seas

darkness descends three-fourths the year,

I stare at cold stars.

Frost-wind, ice-trolled journey,

trusted thanes about the ring-lord,

no man's right is more—

worthiness of woe.

JOHN THE BAPTIST

Fire eyes raised to the red orb,

Quickened

he strode the barren vast,

hot sand moved by roughened feet

setting puffs of dust to dry air.

Faster,

white boiling miraging heat

beneath red sun,

playing heat

in Vitus dance.

On

to the blue cool,

on

to the shoe unloosed,

on

to the fate-full, exquisite face.

OF IVAN KARAMAZOV

Imagine this:

golden Hyperion

steps from his car—

and eases down for peaceful sleep,

giving the watch to black-robed Nyx

as he has time out of mind.

But Nyx—

where is she?

Sleeping still,

sleeping darkly.

Then take one hand

and hold the other—

for you have seen into Ivan's dream.

CECROPS

Drink, dark clouds,

from the silver pools on Parnassus'

summit,

where secrets writhe in caves and hollows

silent—and awe-full.

Drink as the earth rumbles

gulp the ancient ferment

that fattens time's belly;

soon the weights will level

and the sea clap the shore.

Now roar from within,

fling the bright, rampant swords,

let golden rain

soak the faces of the crusted rocks.

HECATE

At the crossways

breathes

an ancient mystery,

an old one,

the Dark One,

whose black eyes

and black hair

haunt the silver night.

TO MY HUSBAND

When the westerly touches your hair
in calm caress,
think of me,
close your eyes,
and see the thread
of golden gossamer
that binds your hand to mine,
we are the one that became two,
the self that said, "I am—
and will be,"
see your face in the silver sea
and gaze on mine.

About the Author

In addition to poetry, Flossie Benton Rogers writes dark paranormal fantasy and is known for conjuring the magic in romance. Former library director and teacher. Essential Energy Balancing and Reiki master, metaphysical tools such as runes, tarot, and crystals. Passionate about comparative mythology, ancient mysteries, true love, and alternate realities. Mystic adventurer. Coffee aficionado. Bedazzled thrall of Marigold the fur fae.

Connect with her at:
FlossieBentonRogers.com

Dark Fantasy Romances
by Flossie Benton Rogers:

Wytchfae Runes
Guardian of the Deep – Wytchfae 2
Mind Your Goddess – Wytchfae 3
Time Singer – Wytchfae 4
Lord of Fire – Wytchfae 5
Demoness Dreams – Wytchfae 6
Soul Weaver – Wytchfae 7

PRINT ANTHOLOGIES:
Dark Guardians
Dark Warriors

www.ingramcontent.com/pod-product-compliance
Lightning Source LLC
Chambersburg PA
CBHW061956040426
42447CB00010B/1781